Contents

Round the world cookbook

Jane Asher

This book tells you how to make exciting food that is eaten in different countries around the world.

KT-555-500

Read this page and page 3 before you make anything.
Remember to read each recipe all the way through before you start.

Some of the recipes need ready-made bread crumbs and pastry.
Some need grated cheese, chopped onion, parsley, or boiled rice.

How to read the recipes

Recipe is the name for the instructions. It tells you how to make something to eat.

On each page, there is a list of the food you will need to have ready.

This list is called Ingredients.

Next comes a list of the things you will have to use, like knives and bowls. This is called Utensils.

On the next page come the instructions. They tell you what to do with the ingredients.

This is called Method.

How to use the recipes

1 Always wash your hands before you start to cook.

2 Measure out all the ingredients before you start.

3 If you are going to cook, turn on the oven first.

4 Cooking can be very dangerous. Always make sure:

- that a grown-up is watching you;

- that you are especially careful when using sharp knives, saucepans and hot cookers.

5 When you have finished, wash everything up and put it away.

Symbols in this book

 This symbol tells you to take extra care. Make sure a grown-up is watching you.

 This symbol tells you to put on oven gloves.

How to prepare some foods

How to grate cheese

⚠️ Mind your fingers!

How to make breadcrumbs

⚠️ Mind your fingers!

How to wash salad

How to separate eggs

1 Have ready a cup or small bowl.

2 Carefully tap the egg on the side of the bowl to crack it.

3 Hold the egg over the bowl and pull it gently into two halves. Do not let the yolk slip into the bowl.

4 Gently tip the yolk from one half of the shell into the other and back again. Let the white part drain off into the bowl/.

5 You will have just the yolk left in the shell.

⚠️

How to boil rice

1 Half fill a large saucepan with water.

2 Bring the water to the boil.

3 Add the rice and boil the water again.

4 Turn down the heat and cover the pan.

5 After about 20 to 30 minutes, the rice will be soft. Pour it into a sieve to drain off the water.

Tuna salad sandwich

My American sister-in-law (my brother's wife) showed me how to make a Tuna salad sandwich the American way.

I thought it was really weird to put Branston pickle into it. Once I tasted it I decided it was a very good idea!

Makes 4

Ingredients

Utensils

plastic sieve

tin opener

medium mixing bowl

tablespoon

fork

table knife

chopping board

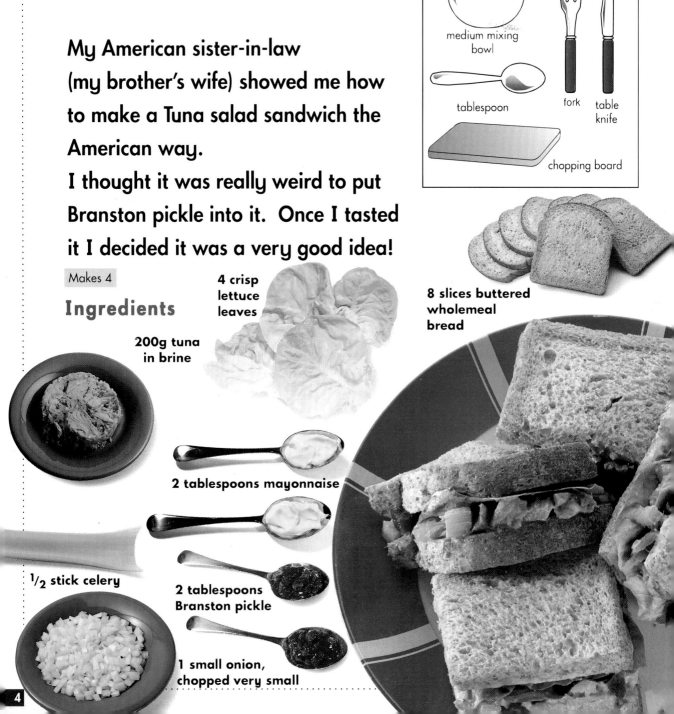

8 slices buttered wholemeal bread

4 crisp lettuce leaves

200g tuna in brine

2 tablespoons mayonnaise

2 tablespoons Branston pickle

½ stick celery

1 small onion, chopped very small

Method

1 Get a grown-up to help you open the tin of tuna. Drain off the liquid down the sink.

2 Put the tuna into the mixing bowl.

3 Chop the celery into small pieces on the chopping board.

4 Add the chopped celery and onion to the bowl of tuna.

5 Add the pickle and mayonnaise. Mix everything together with the fork.

6 Spread the tuna mixture thickly over each of four slices of bread.

7 Put a lettuce leaf on top of the tuna mixture. Cover with another slice of bread.

8 Put each sandwich on to the chopping board. Carefully cut it in half.

Village salad
Χωριάτικη

Salads are made all over the world. What makes the Greek ones so special is the way they add lumps of their lovely, salty feta cheese. Mixing the vegetables with the oil and lemon juice is called 'tossing the salad'.

Utensils

small bowl

chopping board

fork

big bowl

lemon squeezer

vegetable knife

table spoon

8 black olives without stones

112 g feta cheese

1 chopped onion

Serves 4-6

Ingredients

1 green pepper

4 tomatoes

pinch of salt

2 tablespoons olive oil

juice of ¹/₂ lemon

¹/₂ crispy lettuce

Method

1

Put the olive oil, lemon juice and a pinch of salt into the small bowl. Mix together with the fork.

2

⚠️ Wash the pepper. Put it onto the chopping board and carefully cut off the top.

3

⚠️ Pull out the seeds and white pith with your fingers. Cut the pepper into rings and put them into the big bowl.

4

⚠️ Wash the lettuce and tomatoes (see page 3). Cut them into small pieces and put them into the big bowl.

5

Add the chopped pepper and onion to the bowl. Pour in the lemon and oil mixture.

6

Use the spoon and fork to gently cover all the salad with the oil and lemon juice.

7

Cut the cheese into cubes and add to the salad.

8

Mix the cheese in gently so it does not break. Add the olives.

Bureccas

These pastry triangles are filled with cheese. They are very easy to make. Use ready-made puff pastry for them. Eat the bureccas while they are hot - but mind you don't burn your tongue on the cheese inside!

Ingredients

Serves 6

Utensils

small bowl

cup

pastry brush

big bowl

rolling pin

knife   fork

dessertspoon

baking tray

2 eggs

100g feta cheese

50g grated cheddar cheese (see page 2)

flour for rolling out pastry

500g puff pastry

100g half-fat cream cheese

pinch of pepper

sesame seeds or poppy seeds

Method

1 Turn the oven on to 200 deg C/400 deg F.

2 Separate the eggs. Put the whites into the small bowl and the yolks into the big bowl.

3 Add the three types of cheese to the yolks. Sprinkle a pinch of pepper over the top.

4 Break up the feta with a fork and squish the cream cheese until no large lumps are left.

5 Sprinkle the work surface with flour . Roll out the pastry until it is 36cm x 24cm. Cut it into 6 squares.

6 Put a spoonful of the cheese mixture into the middle of each square.

7 Damp 2 edges of each square with the brush. Fold to make a triangle. Press the edges.

8 Put the squares on a greased baking tray. Brush them with egg white.

9 Sprinkle with the seeds. Bake for about 25 minutes until golden brown. Use oven gloves.

Egg fried rice

蛋治炒飯

Rice is the most important food in many parts of the world. There are several different kinds of rice. You can add all sorts of ingredients to rice to make different dishes. I often make this simple recipe for my children.

Serves 4-6

Ingredients

Utensils

small bowl

cup

frying pan

fork

tablespoon

wooden spoon

teaspoon

pinch of salt

pinch of pepper

pinch of sugar

2 tablespoons light soya sauce

2 eggs

1 tablespoon cooking oil

1 cup cooked peas

3 cups boiled rice (see page 3)

1 chopped onion

Method

Break the eggs into the bowl.

Beat the egg yolks and whites together with a fork.

⚠ Put the frying pan on to a medium heat. Carefully add the oil and let it get hot (but not too hot).

⚠ Add the onion. Stir around with the wooden spoon until it looks a bit see-through. Be careful of the hot oil spitting.

Add the rice and peas. Stir until they are hot.

⚠ Sprinkle on the soya sauce and a pinch of salt, sugar and pepper. Stir for a little longer.

⚠ Add the beaten egg to the frying pan. Stir the rice for 2 to 3 minutes and then serve.

Meatballs

Köfte

These are like little hamburgers. In Turkey each cook makes them into his or her own special shape. It would be fun to choose a shape of your own too. Turkish people don't add salt or pepper but you might like to add them.

Makes 9

Ingredients

Utensils

frying pan

teaspoon

dessertspoon

cup

fork

tablespoon

spatula

big mixing bowl

1 teaspoon cumin

1 dessertspoon cooking oil

1 cup breadcrumbs (see page 2)

1 medium chopped onion

1 egg

2 tablespoons chopped parsley

225g lean minced beef

Method

1

Put everything except the cooking oil into the mixing bowl.

2

Mix it all together with a fork.

3

When the mixture sticks together you can knead it with your hands to make it smooth.

4

Pull pieces off the mixture. They will be about the size of ping-pong balls.

5

Flatten the balls. Then make them round, sausage-shape or any other shape you like.

6

⚠ Put the frying pan on to a medium heat. Add the oil and let it get hot.

7

⚠ Use the spatula to put the meat balls into the pan. Be careful in case the hot oil spits out of the pan.

8

⚠ Fry the meat balls for about 5 minutes on each side.

Green bananas

Matoke

I have often seen green bananas in the markets but I have never tried them before writing this book. In Uganda, people eat boiled bananas almost every day. Sometimes they add tomato and onion as in this recipe. Sometimes they add a peanut sauce.

Serves 4-6

Ingredients

Utensils

kitchen knife

chopping board

saucepan

measuring jug

colander

big bowl

5-6 green bananas

2-3 tomatoes

1 chopped onion

pinch of salt

Method

1 Carefully slice down the length of each banana. Cut off the top.

2 Peel the bananas.

3 Cut them into thick slices.

4 Chop the tomatoes into bite-size pieces.

5 Put about 300ml water into the saucepan with a pinch of salt.

6 Put the chopped bananas, tomatoes and onion into the water.

7 Bring the water to the boil (you will see it start to bubble).

8 Let the water boil gently for about 15 minutes or until everything is soft.

9 Put the colander over the sink. Drain off the water. Serve the bananas hot.

Bangladeshi bread

বাংলাদেশী রুটি

Some bread takes a long time to make. This recipe is very simple and great fun - but you will get quite sticky! It is delicious eaten at tea time with some butter and honey or jam.

Makes 6

Ingredients

2 eggs

Utensils

small bowl

measuring jug

fork   teaspoon   big bowl

tablespoon

wooden spoon

baking tray

1 1/2 tablespoons castor sugar

300ml milk

teaspoon of poppy seeds

600g self-raising flour

1 teaspoon baking powder

Method

1 Turn on the oven to 175 deg C/350 deg F.

2 Crack open the eggs and put them into the small bowl. Beat them a little with the fork.

3 Add the milk, sugar and seeds to the eggs. Stir everything together.

4 Put the flour and baking powder into the big bowl. Mix together.

5 Little by little add the milk and eggs mixture to the flour. Keep stirring all the time.

6 When the mixture becomes stiff, put some flour on your hands and mix with them.

7 Keep mixing until the mixture is smooth and firm. Then pull the mixture into 6 pieces.

8 Roll each piece into a ball, then press it flat to make a pancake shape about 1cm thick.

9 Put the bread on to the greased baking tray. Bake for about 15 minutes.

Caribbean fruit salad

You can buy all sorts of exotic fruits in the shops and markets in this country. They are quite expensive so this sort of delicious fruit salad will have to be for special occasions.

Serves 4-6

Ingredients

Utensils

big bowl
lemon squeezer
dessertspoon
peeler
tablespoon
kitchen knife
chopping board

2 ripe mangoes

1 papaya

4 eating apples

2 pink grapefruit

1 tablespoon soft brown sugar

Method

1

Wash all the fruit.

2

⚠ Peel the mangoes. Cut the flesh away from the stone.

3

⚠ Peel the papaya and cut it in half. Scoop out the seeds and white pith with the spoon.

4

⚠ Cut the apples into quarters. Cut out the cores.

5

⚠ Peel one grapefruit and break it into segments. Take off the white pith.

6

⚠ Chop all this fruit into bite-size pieces. Put them in the bowl.

7

Mix all the fruit together gently.

8

⚠ Cut the other grapefruit in half. Squeeze the juice out of it. Add the juice to the fruit.

9

Sprinkle the sugar over the fruit. Stir gently. Put it in a cool place for 2 to 3 hours.

Lassi

This is a wonderfully refreshing drink.
It is especially good if you have it
while you are eating a spicy
meal like curry.
There are different ways
of flavouring the lassi.
This recipe is quite sweet
but you can make it salty
instead if you like.
To do this, leave out
the sugar and add a
couple of pinches
of salt instead.

Serves 6

Ingredients

pinch of saffron

300ml natural yoghurt

juice of one lemon

50g castor sugar

1 litre water

Method

1

Empty the yoghurt into the jug.

2

Beat the yoghurt well with the wooden spoon.

3

Add the water and sugar.

4

Stir until you can't feel any gritty bits. This means the sugar is dissolved.

5

Add the saffron and the lemon juice. Mix it well again with the spoon.

6

Pour it carefully into glasses or beakers.

7

Put one ice cube in each glass.

ice cubes

Add: To add something means you put it into the container with the other ingredients.

Bake: To bake is to cook something in the oven.

Beat: Beating is done with a fork, whisk or wooden spoon. It's a bit like stirring hard.

Boil: When the liquid begins to bubble then it is boiling.

Brush: Dip the pastry brush into the liquid and brush it over the pastry or whatever you are cooking.

Chop: To chop is to cut something into small pieces.

Cut: Cutting is done with a knife. Cut firmly and keep your fingers well away from the blade.

Dissolve: Dissolve is when solids mix with liquids.

Drain: To drain means you put the ingredients into a strainer and let the liquid run out.

Flesh: This is the juicy inside part of a fruit or vegetable.

Fold: You can fold pastry just like you do with paper. It can also mean to mix in gently.

Grease: To grease is to put oil or butter on a tin. This stops the food sticking.

Mix: Mixing can be done using a spoon or fork, you can even use your hands!

Peel: To peel means to take the peel off the outside with a sharp knife or peeler.

Pinch: Pinch a small amount of the ingredient between your finger and thumb.

Pith: This is the white part of fruit that is between the skin and the flesh.

Pour: Pour liquid from a special jug with a lip to stop it spilling.

Roll: Sprinkle the work surface with flour before you roll out pastry to stop it sticking.

Scoop: To scoop is to take the inside out of something with a spoon.

Slice: To slice is to cut something into flat sections. These can be thick or thin.

Squeeze: You can squeeze the juice out of fruit using your hand or a special squeezer.

Squish: My word for using a fork to break up food into a mush.

Spread: Use a table knife or a spatula for spreading.

Stir: To stir is to mix with a spoon. Use a wooden spoon if you are stirring something hot, as the spoon will stay cool.

Wash: Rub fruit and vegetables gently with your fingers under cold water.